Pterosaurs
Up Close

Flying Reptiles

Peter
Dodson, PhD

Zoom In on Dinosaurs!

Illustrated by John Bindon

CONTENTS

WORDS TO KNOW

crest—A thin piece of bone on top of the head.

dinosaurs (DY noh sorz)—Reptiles that lived from about 230 million years ago to 65 million years ago. They had a special kind of hip and long legs.

fossils (FAH sulz)—Parts of living things from long ago. They are often turned to stone.

mosasaur (MOH zuh sor)—A reptile that lived in the sea during the age of dinosaurs.

plesiosaur (PLEE zee uh sor)—A reptile that lived in the sea during the age of dinosaurs.

pterosaur (TAIR uh sor)—A flying reptile that lived during the age of dinosaurs. Pterosaurs were not dinosaurs.

Pronunciation Guide

Ctenochasma [TEEN oh KAZ muh]

Dsungaripterus [JUNG gar IP tur us]

Pteranodon [teh RAN uh don]

Pterodactylus [TAIR uh DAK tih lus]

Pterodaustro [TAIR uh DOS troh]

Quetzalcoatlus [KET zahl koh AT lus]

Rhamphorhynchus [RAM foh RING kus]

The Flying Reptiles

Pterosaurs flew in the sky.

They flew over the heads of **dinosaurs**.

But pterosaurs were not dinosaurs.

They were reptiles that were cousins of dinosaurs.

Their bones were hollow and thin.

Pteranodon

Pterodactylus

Dsungaripterus

Ctenochasma

Pterodaustro

Many Kinds of Pterosaurs

The word *pterosaur* means "wing reptile."

There were many different kinds of pterosaurs.

Some pterosaurs were small like sparrows.

Others were the size of small airplanes.

Quetzalcoatlus

Rhamphorhynchus

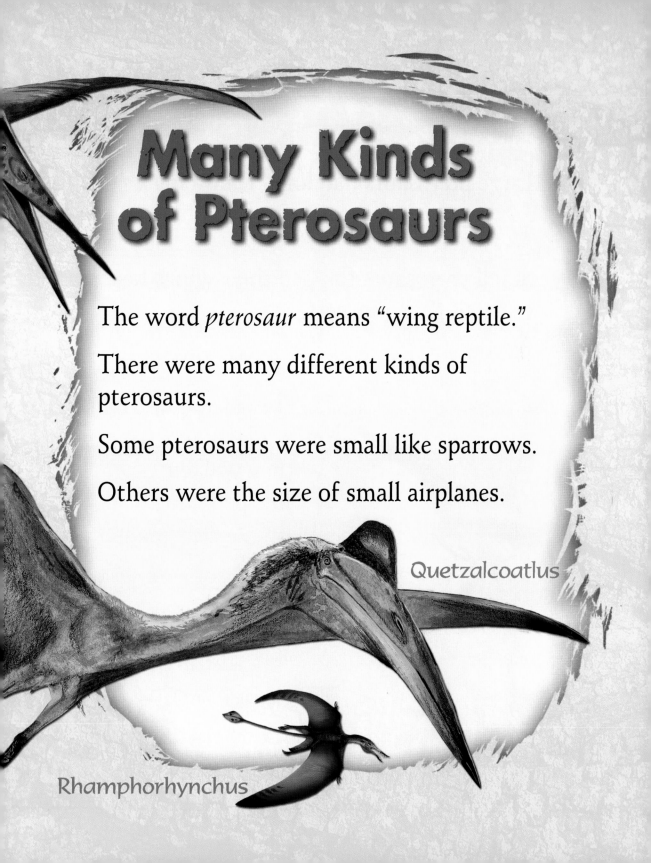

Wings

Large pterosaurs had long, thin wings.

They glided over the seas.

Small pterosaurs flapped their wings fast to catch flying insects.

On the ground, they folded their wings.

Pterosaurs probably waddled when they walked, like penguins.

9

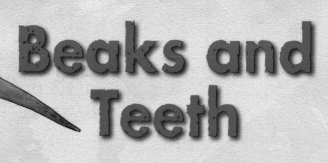

Beaks and Teeth

All pterosaurs had long beaks.

Many had long pointy teeth.

Some had short round teeth.

Some had no teeth at all.

Some had **crests** on the snout, above the eyes, or at the back of the head.

Tails

Some of the first pterosaurs had long bony tails.

Rhamphorhynchus had a diamond shape at the end of its tail.

It helped this reptile steer through the air.

Other kinds of pterosaurs had no tails at all.

14

What's for Dinner?

Pterosaurs found their food in lakes or in shallow seas.

They ate many kinds of food.

They really liked to eat fish.

Some ate animals with hard shells, such as snails, clams, and crabs.

Some ate small shrimp from the water.

Some caught insects that flew over the water.

Growing Up

Pterosaurs hatched from eggs.

Some egg **fossils** have been found.

One leathery egg found in China was two inches long.

It had a baby pterosaur folded inside!

Scientists could finally see what a baby pterosaur looked like.

Pterosaurs took several years to grow to full size.

Skin

Pterosaurs did not have feathers.
Their skin was leathery like a bat's.

A few fossils show that hairy fuzz
grew on their skin.

One type of pterosaur was called
Ctenochasma. It ate small pink shrimp.
That's what flamingos eat.
It makes them pink.

Maybe *Ctenochasma*
was pink like a
flamingo!

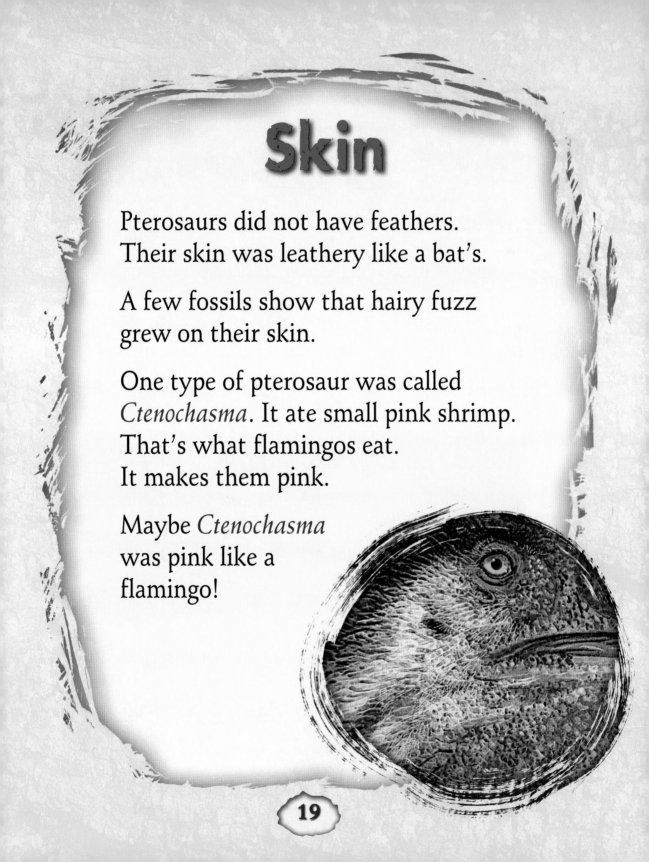

Pterosaurs Were Not Alone

Pterosaurs flew over seas.

The seas were filled with fish and turtles.

Pterosaurs had to stay away from the snapping jaws of long-necked **plesiosaurs** and **mosasaurs** in the water.

On land, some brave pterosaurs may have rested on the backs of gentle, long-necked dinosaurs.

Where on Earth?

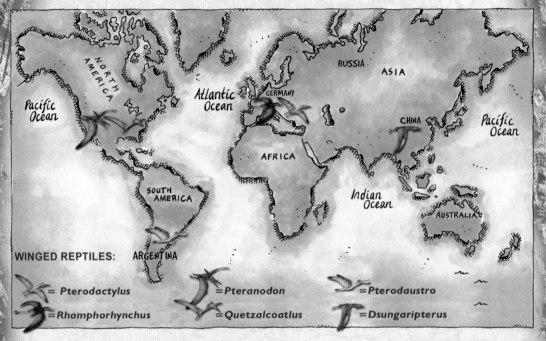

WINGED REPTILES:

= Pterodactylus   = Pteranodon   = Pterodaustro

= Rhamphorhynchus   = Quetzalcoatlus   = Dsungaripterus

Pterosaur fossils have been found almost everywhere on earth. The fossils show scientists where pterosaurs used to live.

Very famous pterosaurs such as *Pterodactylus* and *Rhamphorhynchus* lived in Germany. *Pteranodon* and giant *Quetzalcoatlus* lived in the United States. *Pterodaustro* lived in Argentina. *Dsungaripterus* lived in China.

Learn More

Books

Arnold, Caroline. *Pterosaurs: Rulers of the Skies in the Dinosaur Age*. New York: Clarion, 2004.

Ashby, Ruth. *Pteranodon: The Life Story of a Pterosaur*. New York: Harry N. Abrahams, 2005.

Landau, Elaine. *Pterosaurs*. New York: Scholastic, 2007.

Web Sites

El Nabli, Dina. "Found: Flying Reptile Fossil!" *Time For Kids*. <http://www.timeforkids.com/TFK/kids/news/story/0,28277,326274,00.html>

Enchanted Learning. *Zoom Dinosaurs*. <http://www.enchantedlearning.com/subjects/dinosaurs>

INDEX

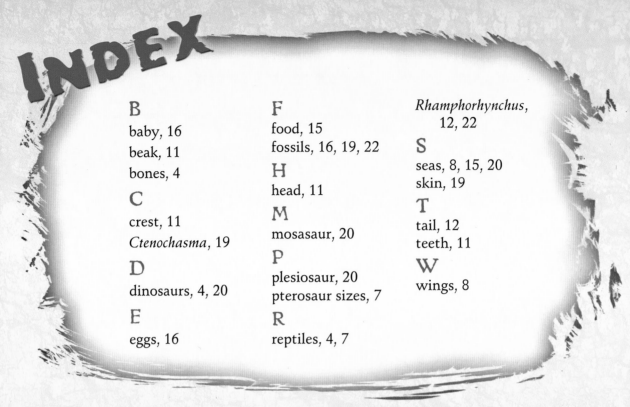

For Jonah Emile

Bailey Books, an imprint of Enslow Publishers, Inc.

Copyright © 2011 by Peter Dodson

All rights reserved.

No part of this book may be reproduced by any means without the written permission of the publisher.

Library of Congress Cataloging-in-Publication Data

Dodson, Peter.
Pterosaurs up close : flying reptiles / by Peter Dodson.
    p. cm. — (Zoom in on dinosaurs!)
Summary: "Gives young readers an up-close look at pterosaurs and how their features helped them live"—Provided by publisher.
Includes bibliographical references and index.
ISBN 978-0-7660-3332-0
1. Pterosauria—Juvenile literature. I. Title.
QE862.P7D63 2011
567.918—dc22   2009021275

062010 Lake Book Manufacturing, Inc., Melrose Park, IL

Printed in the United States of America

10 9 8 7 6 5 4 3 2 1

Illustration Credits: John Bindon

Cover Illustration: John Bindon

To Our Readers: We have done our best to make sure all Internet Addresses in this book were active and appropriate when we went to press. However, the author and the publisher have no control over and assume no liability for the material available on those Internet sites or on other Web sites they may link to. Any comments or suggestions can be sent by e-mail to comments@enslow.com or to the address on the back cover.

Note to Parents and Teachers: The *Zoom In on Dinosaurs!* series supports the National Science Education Standards for K–4 science. The Words to Know section introduces subject-specific vocabulary words, including pronunciation and definitions. Early readers may need help with these new words.

Allan A. De Fina, PhD
Series Literacy Consultant
Dean, College of Education
Professor of Literacy Education
New Jersey City University
Past President of the New Jersey Reading Association

Philip J. Currie, PhD
Series Science Consultant
Professor of Dinosaur Paleobiology
University of Alberta
Edmonton, Alberta
Canada

Bailey Books
an imprint of
Enslow Publishers, Inc.
40 Industrial Road
Box 398
Berkeley Heights, NJ 07922
USA
http://www.enslow.com